HEAR OUR STORIES

By Sharon Stewart

CELEBRATION PRESS
Pearson Learning Group

The following people from **Pearson Learning Group**
have contributed to the development of this product:

Joan Mazzeo, Dorothea Fox **Design** | **Editorial** Leslie Feierstone-Barna, Cindy Kane
Christine Fleming **Marketing** | **Publishing Operations** Jennifer Van Der Heide
Production Laura Benford-Sullivan
Content Area Consultant Dr. Daniel J. Gelo

The following people from **DK** have
contributed to the development of this product:

Art Director Rachael Foster

Martin Wilson **Managing Art Editor** | **Managing Editor** Marie Greenwood
Wilfrid Wood **Design** | **Editorial** Julie Ferris
Sarah Duncan, Frances Vargo **Picture Research** | **Production** Gordana Simakovic
Richard Czapnik, Andy Smith **Cover Design** | **DTP** David McDonald
Consultant Joseph Bruchac

Dorling Kindersley would like to thank: Lucy Heaver for editorial assistance. Rose Horridge, Gemma Woodward, and Hayley Smith in the DK Picture Library. Johnny Pau for additional cover design work.

Picture Credits: Bridgeman Art Library, London/New York: Corbally Stourton Contemporary Art, London UK 11. Corbis: Yann Arthus-Bertrand 28t; Asian Art & Archaeology, Inc. 26br; Kevin Fleming 14bl; Honetchurch Antiques, Ltd. 27tr; George H. H. Huey 15tr; DiMaggio/Kalish 24b; Catherine Karnow 3; Charles & Josette Lenars 7t, 12bl; Viviane Moos 1; Pat O'Hara 14tr; Bob Rowan/Progressive Image 17bl; DK Images: British Museum 16tr; © CONACULTA-INAH-MEX. Authorized reproduction by the Instituto Nacional de Antropologia e Historia 18cr; South Australian Museum Assembling the Totem, by a Melville Island artist 12tr; Wallace Collection 30bl. Mary Evans Picture Library: 6bl, 29bl. FLPA – Images of nature: Martin Withers 10b. Werner Forman Archive: 7cr; Museum Fur Volkerkunde, Hamburg 19tl; National Museum, Copenhagen 28br; Schindler Collection, New York 17tr. Robert Harding Picture Library: Robert Frerck/Odyssey/Chicago 24tr. © Michael Holford: 5, 6cr. Katz/FSP: Beijing Jin Chenn 27bl. Lonely Planet Images: Rick Gerharter 20bl. National Geographic Image Collection: Sam Abell 13t. Panos Pictures: Jeremy Hartley 9tr. South American Pictures: Tony Morrision 20tr. Courtesy of Pat Speight: 31cr. The Photolibrary Wales: Steve Benbow 31t. Jacket: Panos Pictures: front t; Jeremy Hartley front bl. Corbis: Pat O'Hara back.

All other images: DK Dorling Kindersley © 2005. For further information see www.dkimages.com

For information regarding licensing and permissions, write to Rights and Permissions Department, Pearson Learning Group, 299 Jefferson Road, Parsippany, NJ 07054 USA or to Rights and Permissions Department, DK Publishing, The Penguin Group (UK), 80 Strand, London WC2R ORL.

Lexile is a U.S. registered trademark of MetaMetrics, Inc. All rights reserved.

ISBN: 0-7652-5261-9

Color reproduction by Colourscan, Singapore
Printed in the United States of America.
2 3 4 5 6 7 8 9 10   08 07 06 05

1-800-321-3106
www.pearsonlearning.com

Contents

Introduction

A murmur of voices weaves a web of stories around the world. This web is the oral tradition—stories told by word of mouth. Since early times, people in every culture have passed stories down from one generation to the next. Every time you tell a joke, quote a proverb, or recite a poem, you are part of this oral tradition.

Tales From Mouth to Ear

Stories are perhaps the most important part of the oral tradition. Long before writing was invented, people told tales to explain events in the world, to keep track of history, and to entertain others. These tales were passed from one person to another. The story lines stayed the same, but the details changed a little with every telling.

The invention of writing did not stop the telling of tales because for a long time, very few people could read. Many people also enjoyed hearing the sounds of language itself as a story was told. For hundreds of years, storytellers were the historians, entertainers, and keepers of truths in their communities. In many cultures, they still are.

A storyteller entertains a group of students in London, England.

CHARACTERISTICS OF TRADITIONAL TALES

	Myth	Legend	Folk Tales
Type of Story	sacred or religious story from the past	tale of adventure or hero; may be true but exaggerated	wonder story with fantastic events
Purpose	to explain the unknown	to entertain or tell about the past	to entertain or give examples or advice about how to act
Characters	gods, goddesses, supernatural characters	heroes who may have lived in the past	some characters are realistic, others are fantastic
Examples	origin stories, creation stories	epic sagas	wonder tales, fairy tales

Kinds of Traditional Tales

Most of the stories that have been told generation after generation were eventually written down. Every culture has these timeless stories. Some tell of the creation of the world and of human beings. Others describe how things came to be or explain the meaning of life and death.

On Easter Island, a bird-man represents the creator god.

Many tales from different cultures have similar characteristics. Myths are one type of tale. They are sacred or religious stories from the past. Many myths try to explain the unknown, such as the origin of life and the creation of the world. Characters in myths are often gods and goddesses with supernatural powers. Myths are not realistic stories, yet they share deep truths about human nature and the world around us.

Legends are also popular. These stories tell of the adventures of heroes who may have lived in the past. Their achievements, however, are usually larger than life. Legends may also tell about real places or events.

Folk tales are popular traditional stories. These stories are wonder tales—stories of fun and fancy or high adventure that everyone understands are make-believe. Most traditional stories from every culture can be categorized as myths, legends, or folk tales. Read on to discover the similarities and differences among traditional stories from all over the world.

The mask above was worn in African tribal dances to impersonate the cunning Hare (left), a character in many African stories. In North America, this trickster figure became known as Brer Rabbit.

||| ≡ ||| ≡|||≡ |||≡ ||| ≡ |||≡|||≡|||

The Dogon people of Mali wear masks to represent the creator god Amma in dances.

African Stories

Africa's story traditions are as varied as its cultures and peoples. Yet many of the stories have similar characters and themes. They include a creator god, a world serpent, animal tricksters, and twins.

Creation Myths

There are hundreds of African cultures, and each has a different story of how the universe began. Many African creation stories begin with a god or gods who emerge from an egg. Some creation stories involve twins.

Most often, African creation myths include a supreme god. This god begins by making the world, then leaves others in charge. The people of the Dahomey region in West Africa believe that the creator god Mawu was carried in the mouth of a rainbow serpent called Aido-Hwedo. Rivers and valleys twist and curve because that was how Aido-Hwedo moved. When Mawu finished creating Earth, she realized that it was too heavy, and Aido-Hwedo was told to coil himself into a circle for Earth to rest on.

The Edo people of Nigeria believe a python was the god of the sea's messenger.

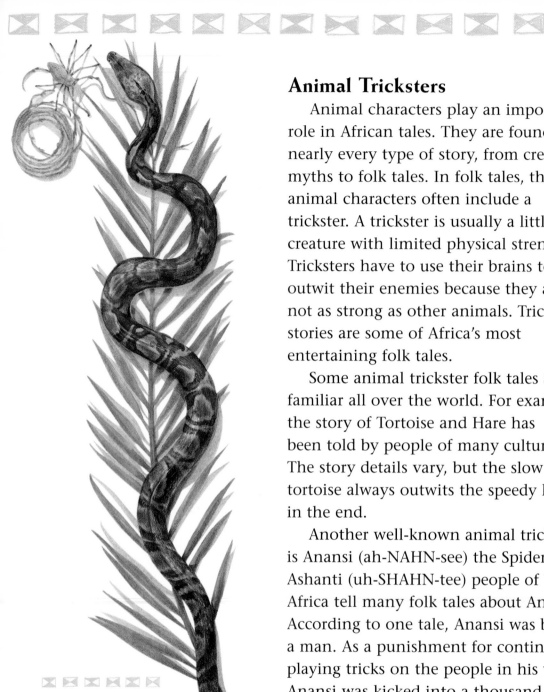

Animal Tricksters

Animal characters play an important role in African tales. They are found in nearly every type of story, from creation myths to folk tales. In folk tales, the animal characters often include a trickster. A trickster is usually a little creature with limited physical strength. Tricksters have to use their brains to outwit their enemies because they are not as strong as other animals. Trickster stories are some of Africa's most entertaining folk tales.

Some animal trickster folk tales are familiar all over the world. For example, the story of Tortoise and Hare has been told by people of many cultures. The story details vary, but the slow tortoise always outwits the speedy hare in the end.

Another well-known animal trickster is Anansi (ah-NAHN-see) the Spider. The Ashanti (uh-SHAHN-tee) people of West Africa tell many folk tales about Anansi. According to one tale, Anansi was born a man. As a punishment for continually playing tricks on the people in his village, Anansi was kicked into a thousand pieces. Storytellers explain that all those pieces were put back together into a spider.

Anansi is always very entertaining because of his cunning tricks—he was even able to trick the gods!

✕ ✕ ✕ ✕ ✕

In one Ashanti tale, Anansi captures a python. He tricks the snake into stretching along a palm branch and then ties him up.

Telling African Stories

African storytellers told tales under the shade of trees or around village fires. They often enhanced their stories with drumming, songs, and dances. These storytellers passed on messages from the rulers of the land. They memorized cultural and family histories and often used their stories to show people how to solve problems.

Griots and *griottes* have been performing for nearly a thousand years.

Traditional South African Zulu dancing tells stories through movement.

Storytelling is still alive and well in Africa today. Traditional entertainment in Senegal (sen-uh-GAHL) usually includes male and female storytellers called *griots* and *griottes* (both pronounced GREE-ohz) who sing, dance, tell stories and jokes, and play their instruments. *Griots* and *griottes* are part of modern life. Today, they often add amplifiers to their instruments and travel to new places to entertain new audiences.

Storytelling thrives in other parts of Africa, too. In South Africa, for example, a group called Zanendaba (zan-en-DAH-buh) Storytellers is teaching a new generation of storytellers. They will continue the oral tradition.

Australian Aboriginal Stories

The culture of the Aboriginal peoples of Australia is rich in storytelling. Aboriginal mythology preserves ideas from ancient times. Aboriginal peoples have lived in Australia for more than 60,000 years. Rock paintings of their mythological story characters date back 6,000 to 8,000 years.

According to a myth of one group of Australian Aboriginals, Bobbi-bobbi, the rainbow snake, used one of his ribs to make the boomerang.

The Dreamtime

Aboriginal stories relate to a period called the Dreamtime. This is a mystical time when it is said that the sacred ancestors of the Aboriginal peoples came to Earth and shaped the world. These myths explain how the land, people, plants, and animals were created. The myths say that the ancestor spirits traveled about the land. As they traveled, they stopped at certain places to form mountains and rivers.

Dreamtime stories also explain that when the ancestor spirits finished their work, they turned themselves into objects in nature, such as animals, stars, plants, and hills. To the Aboriginal peoples of Australia, the Dreamtime is real and all around them; their ancestors are still present in the natural world they created.

One of the Dreamtime myths is about Uluru (OOL-uh-roo), the great red sandstone monolith in the desert of central Australia.

Tales of the Dreamtime

One Aboriginal story tells how an ancestor spirit named Guthi-guthi helped bring water to the land. Because the land was bare and nothing grew, he asked the water serpent Weowie (WEE-oh-wee) to help him. Guthi-guthi stood on a mountain and called and called, but Weowie was trapped under a mountain and didn't hear him. Eventually Guthi-guthi became so angry that he banged on the mountain until it split apart. Weowie escaped and traveled across the land making waterholes and streams wherever he went.

Another Dreamtime tale explains how two mountains and an island along the south coast of New South Wales of Australia were created. Gulaga (GOO-lah-gah), one of these coastal mountains,

Snakes feature in many Dreamtime stories. In one story, a snake bites the Sun, creating the first sunset. In another, a giant python forms rivers as she crosses the landscape.

is called the "mother mountain" by the Aboriginal peoples. The tale explains that Gulaga had two sons, Barranguba (bah-rahn-GOO-buh) and Najanuga (nah-jan-NOO-guh).

Barranguba, the older son, asked his mother if he could go out alone to the sea and watch the fish and whales. Gulaga let him go, but she told Najanuga that he could not go with his brother because he was too young. Today, the mountain Najanuga stands near Gulaga on the coast while Barranguba is an island in the sea, surrounded by fish and whales.

How the Tales Are Told

The Aboriginal peoples of every region of Australia have their own stories. By custom, the tales are told sitting around a campfire. Some stories are secret and sacred and cannot be told to non-Aboriginal people. Some are tales for women or men only. Some storytellers accompany their tales with drawings made on a section of sand.

Many Aboriginal myths are recorded as art. These include paintings on rocks, tree bark, and people's faces and bodies. Special symbols and designs are said to pass on the power of the ancestors and help tell the Dreamtime stories.

To make bark paintings, Aboriginal artists strip layers of bark from trees, scrape them, dry them over a fire, and flatten them under weights.

Australian Aboriginals continue to tell stories in the traditional way.

Telling the Tales Today

In Australia and the Torres Strait Islands, there are many different groups of indigenous peoples. Each group has its own versions of the Dreamtime stories. The people chosen to be storytellers are respected members of their groups. Traditionally, Aboriginal storytellers are born into the role because their parents were storytellers. However, others can also earn the right to tell stories. The stories are told to entertain and to teach history, culture, and values. A five-minute story may have twenty different lessons in it. Children may understand some of the lessons, whereas the deeper meanings are for the adults.

In the past, Aboriginal storytellers told stories of their own people and place. Storytellers now tell stories of different places in Australia. Aboriginal elders have permitted some stories to be made public. These stories are retold on television, on CD, at storytelling festivals, and in schools. Dreamtime stories are now enjoyed by people throughout the world.

Aboriginal storytellers are respected and popular performers.

Native American Stories

Like African and Australian Aboriginal stories, Native American tales do more than entertain. They explain the world. They also show how to live in harmony with others and with nature.

The Creation Myths

There are many different Native American creation myths; however, most describe three worlds: the upper world, which is made of light; the earthly world; and the lower world, which is made of darkness.

Animals act as creators, messengers, protectors, guardians, and advisors in many myths. The coyote, bear, raven, spider, and turtle often serve as spiritual guides or important members of the community.

The Cherokee (CHER-uh-kee) creation myth says the world was once a great sea held by four ropes—the four directions. At this time, the animals lived above the sea in a place called Galunlati. A brave little water beetle decided to find out what was below the sea. Again and again, he dived down and brought up mud to form land. Next, Buzzard created Earth's mountains and valleys by flapping his wings on the soft mud. Soon all the animals came down, and they set the Sun in motion to warm their new home.

This Cherokee headband symbolizes the four directions.

Native peoples of the Pacific Northwest carve totem poles to represent the myths related to their clans or families.

Tricksters and Heroes

Of the animal characters that appear in Native American tales, the coyote appears most often. Coyotes are highly respected for their cleverness. In many tales, Coyote is a trickster.

Coyotes are featured in many Native American tales.

In a creation story from the Maidu people, who lived in what is now California, Coyote was with Earthmaker, and they were the first two chiefs. Unfortunately, Earthmaker and Coyote never agreed on anything. Like most tricksters, Coyote made mischief constantly. Earthmaker wanted to kill Coyote, but he couldn't catch him. In the end, Earthmaker just left Coyote alone; however, he warned people to stay away from Coyote because he would always cause trouble.

In Native American tales from the northern and northwestern United States and western Canada, Raven can be a creator figure or a trickster. An Inuit (IN-noo-it) story tells that Raven, or Tulungersak (TOO-lung-uhr-sak), began as a human. He came to Earth and decided to make a figure like himself from clay. This figure was restless and unhappy, though, so Raven threw it away. Next, Raven decided to explore the sky. So he made himself some wings and turned into the first raven. After that, Raven created humans from clay. He taught people how to hunt and fish and he made light and darkness.

In Inuit myth, Raven made human beings, animals, and plants and created light and darkness.

Animals and the Sea

In the past, the Inuit peoples of northern Canada and Greenland depended on animals for food, clothing, and shelter. Because animals were important to the Inuit peoples, they created tales to describe their relationship with animals, their history, and their culture. One of their best-known myths tells about the goddess Sedna, the Mother of the Sea Beasts.

Sedna was once a human girl who married a young man who turned out to be a sea-bird in disguise. Sedna's father tried to rescue her, but as they traveled home in a boat, the sea-bird caused a huge storm to rage. Sedna's father became very frightened, and he threw Sedna overboard as a way to satisfy the sea-bird. When she tried to climb back into the boat, her father grabbed the paddle and pounded against her fingers until they fell off. As Sedna sank to the bottom of the sea, her fingers became seals and all the other sea creatures. Now Sedna rules the underworld and all living things.

This wooden mask shows the sea creatures that belonged to the goddess Sedna.

In the Inuit legend, Sedna sank into the sea.

Telling Native American Tales

Some Native American stories are told only at special times of the year, in certain places, or on important days. Other tales are told to young people by parents and elders as part of daily life. Movement, song, and dance are part of the telling of certain stories. For example, the Inuit people chant and dance their tales to the beat of drums. Some Inuits also use knives to draw pictures in the ground or in the snow to accompany stories. This is called storyknifing.

The Navajo people make sand paintings showing supernatural beings from their stories.

Native American storytellers often visit schools to tell their traditional stories.

The Yukon International Storytelling Festival takes place every year in Whitehorse, a city in Canada's Yukon Territory. It draws storytellers from all over the world. They listen to tales and tell their own stories. Some groups, such as the Zuñis in the American Southwest, also broadcast stories on their own radio stations. These groups want to strengthen the storytelling tradition and ensure that it remains a vital part of teaching Native American history and culture.

Mesoamerican and South American Stories

Long ago, the Maya (MY-uh) and Aztecs (AZ-teks) of Mesoamerica and the Incas of South America created great civilizations. Their myths have survived, even though their civilizations have not.

Myths of the Maya

Between A.D. 250 and 900, the Maya built great stone cities in the heart of the Mesoamerican jungle. They created picture writing and an accurate calendar. The Maya recorded stories mentioning many different gods.

One Maya myth tells of the twin gods Xbalanque (EX-bal-ANK-ay) and Hunahpu (HOO-nah-poo). These twins loved to play a ritual ball game. The other gods, annoyed with the twins because the game was so loud, sent them to play against the lords of the Underworld. The stakes were high: life or death. The twins won the game and cut off the heads of the death gods. Later, the twins became the Sun and the Moon.

In a Maya myth, Chac, a weeping warrior, watered the fields with his tears.

This painted book shows Maya picture writing, which recorded Maya stories.

This carving shows Quetzalcoatl in disguise.

Legends and Myths of the Aztecs

The Aztecs built a powerful empire in Mexico during the fifteenth century. Like the Maya, the Aztecs built cities and temples of stone and used picture writing. Their gods were similar to Maya gods. One famous Aztec myth is about Quetzalcoatl (kets-uhl-KWOT-uhl), the king of the City of Gods. He was a very good god and would never do any harm. One day, another god played a trick on Quetzalcoatl by giving him a human face and body. Quetzalcoatl was so disgusted with his human appearance that he disguised himself as a feathered serpent in a coat of green, red, and white feathers from the quetzal bird.

Quetzalcoatl taught humans important skills such as growing food. He taught them to measure time and understand the stars. One day, Quetzalcoatl sailed away, but the Aztecs believed he would return. When the Spaniards arrived in 1519, the Aztecs believed at first that the Spanish leader Hernán Cortés was Quetzalcoatl.

Quetzalcoatl disguised himself as a serpent.

Inca Myths

The Incas flourished in the fifteenth and sixteenth centuries. Their civilization was based in South America's Andes Mountains. The Incas built wonderful cities and a great road system.

The Inca creator god was Viracocha (vee-ruh-KOH-chuh). First, he made a group of giants, but when they disobeyed him, he sent a flood to drown them. Next, Viracocha created light by raising the Sun, the Moon, and stars from the waters of a lake. Finally, he created human beings out of clay.

This mask shows the power and beauty of Inti, the Inca Sun god.

Inti, the Inca god of the Sun, was the son of Viracocha. Inti sent his own son, Manco Capac, to rule Earth and to teach people how to live. The Inca rulers believed Inti was their ancestor. They used gold, a symbol of the Sun god, to decorate his temples.

Musician-storytellers in Latin America perform *corridos*, or folk songs, that often comment on political events.

Telling the Stories Today

Since the 1990s, storytelling in Mesoamerica and South America has become popular again. Some Mesoamerican and South American storytellers retell ancient myths. Others create new stories based on the modern lifestyles of today's people. Many people believe that the ritual of listening to stories, ancient or modern, is an opportunity to establish new ideas about the world.

Arab Stories

The Arab story tradition is rich in all kinds of tales—romances, historical legends, animal fables, trickster tales, and lesson tales. The most famous of all Arab stories are the wonder tales known as *The Arabian Nights*, or *The Thousand and One Nights*. The stories came from Arabia, India, and Persia, which is now Iran. The stories were told for many centuries before they were written down.

In *The Arabian Nights*, Shahrazad tells King Shahryar a series of stories.

The Tale of King Shahryar and Shahrazad

The stories of *The Arabian Nights* are set within a tale about a noble but cruel king named Shahryar (SHAH-ry-uh). Betrayed by his first wife, he began to marry one young woman after another, killing each one the morning after the wedding. One girl named Shahrazad (SHAH-ruh-zod) decided to stop him. She married him, and on the wedding night she told a tale, breaking off at the most exciting part at dawn. Amazed, King Shahryar spared her life so he could hear the end of the story. This continued night after night for a few years, when the king realized he loved Shahrazad and could never harm her.

Arab fishermen sailed in traditional fishing vessels called *dhows*.

The Tale of the Fisherman and the Genie

The first tale that Shahrazad told King Shahryar was about a poor fisherman who caught a huge copper jar in his net. When he pulled out the jar's cork, a cloud of smoke poured out. The cloud then turned into a fearsome genie. Furious at having been trapped for so long, the genie vowed to kill the fisherman. The fisherman mocked him, saying that one so big could never have fit into such a small jar. To prove him wrong, the genie angrily slipped back in, and the fisherman pushed the stopper back into the jar. He threw the jar back into the sea.

Aladdin and His Wonderful Lamp

Perhaps the best-known tale from
The Arabian Nights is the story of
Aladdin, a poor boy who lived in China.
A magician took him to a magic cave
where Aladdin found an old oil lamp.
The magician demanded the lamp,
but Aladdin refused and kept it.
He discovered that rubbing the lamp
would call a genie to fulfill his wishes.
Aladdin made himself wealthy and
married the emperor's daughter.

One day, the magician came back.
He fooled Aladdin's wife into giving
him the lamp. At once, Aladdin's
palace and his bride vanished.
In the end, Aladdin caught
up with the wicked magician.
He rescued the princess,
took the lamp, and lived
happily ever after.

In the story, Aladdin rubs
a traditional oil lamp.

When Aladdin rubbed
the lamp, a genie appeared.

Arab Storytelling Today

Storytelling is a family activity in many Arab countries. Parents often tell stories to their children. Adults also listen to tales told by professional storytellers. In Syria, storytellers called *hakawati* entertain in cafes. In Egypt, the storyteller is called a *sha'ir* (SHAH-eer), and in Iraq, this entertainer is known as a *qisa khoun* (KEY-suh koon). In some countries, storytellers play on a stringed instrument while they talk.

In Djemaa El-Fna Square, visitors can watch acrobats, snake-charmers, and fire-eaters, as well as listen to stories.

For almost 1,000 years, Djemaa El-Fna (JEEM-uh ELF-nah) Square, near the city of Marrakech (MAHR-uh-kesh) in Morocco, has been a meeting place where people have gathered for storytelling and other street performances. In 2001, the United Nations Educational, Scientific, and Cultural Organization (UNESCO) declared the square a World Heritage Center for oral tradition. Hopefully, stories will be told there in the future.

This Egyptian *sha'ir* is playing a stringed instrument called a *rabbah* (rahb-BAH).

Chinese and Japanese Stories

The ancient civilizations of China and Japan have many tales of gods and heroes. These tales often express the basic ideas of the Buddhist religion in China and the Shinto (SHIN-toh) religion in Japan.

Chinese Myths and Tales

One Chinese creation myth says the world began with a great egg. Yin and yang, the struggling forces inside, split the egg apart. Out came Pan Ku, the creator god. He shaped the world with a hammer and chisel with help from a dragon, a phoenix, a unicorn, a tiger, and a tortoise. After more than 10,000 years, Pan Ku died, but his body became part of the world around us. His skull is the dome of the heavens, his eyes are the Sun and the Moon, and his breath is the wind.

According to the Chinese, the opposing forces yin and yang must be balanced in the universe. Yin, an earth force, is dark, heavy, and cold. Yang, the sky force, is bright, light, and warm.

As in some African myths, the Chinese creator god Pan Ku came from a great egg.

The story of Lung Mo, or Dragon Mother, is another ancient Chinese tale. When Lung Mo found a dragon egg, she kept it warm and eventually raised the dragon as her son. When the emperor tried to imprison Lung Mo, the dragon carried her away to safety on his back. Later, the Chinese made Lung Mo a goddess because she was the only person that a dragon has ever carried on its back.

Japanese Myths and Tales

Shinto is the oldest religion of Japan. The Shinto gods, called *kami*, are the basic force in mountains, rivers, and other parts of nature. The mythology of Shinto also has an explanation for the creation of the world. A Shinto myth explains that two gods, Izanagi (ee-zahn-AH-gee) and Izanami (ee-zahn-AHM-ee), created the world. They created the heavens and many more gods. Then they created the group of islands that became Japan.

The two rocks of Meoto Iwa, in Japan's Shima Peninsula, represent the gods Izanami and Izanagi and are connected by a sacred rope.

Folk tales about tiny children are common all over the world. In the ancient Japanese tale called "Peach Boy," a tiny boy popped out of a peach pit. Once Peach Boy grew up, he wanted to help his family and neighbors. At that time, evil ogres were raiding the villages and harming people. So Peach Boy set off for Ogre Island to stop the ogres.

On his journey, Peach Boy met a dog, a monkey, and a pheasant. They were all fighting among themselves. Peach Boy persuaded them to stop fighting each other and help him fight the ogres. At Ogre Island, Peach Boy and the animals used amusing strategies to make the ogres give up their evil ways.

Peach Boy traveled with three animals.

Storytelling in China and Japan

In China today, stories are told in special story houses. Some storytellers work in pairs. Others tell stories while playing drums, clappers, or stringed instruments. Some stories are traditional. Others include clever comments about modern government and society.

In Japan, storytellers preserved religious myths by singing them at religious festivals. Today, *Nôgaku* (NOH-gah-koo) theater uses masks, music, and dancing to tell traditional stories. The masks show the expressions of the characters, and much of the story is told through movement.

Another tradition of Japanese storytelling is called *kamishibai* (kah-mee-shee-by-ee). These stories were first told by street vendors who struck wooden clappers to gather a crowd. After candies and other snacks had been sold, the story began. The tales were told as serials, to be continued, leaving the audience eager for more.

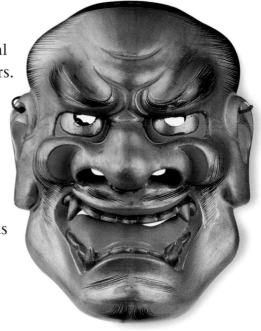

Nôgaku masks depict women, old men, children, and ghosts.

Chinese story-house tales may be about military heroes, outlaws, or Chinese history.

Celtic Stories

The Celts (KELTS) were wandering peoples who finally settled in western Europe. Many of the people lived in small villages and were led by warrior chiefs. The best known Celtic stories come from Great Britain and Ireland.

Celtic Gods and Goddesses

Celtic gods and goddesses are linked to nature and farming. One of the gods was Cernunnos (KER-noo-nohs), also known as the Horned One. This Celtic god had a human body with the ears and antlers of a stag. He was a shape changer and might appear as a stag, a wolf, or a snake. Cernunnos was also the leader of the Wild Hunt, a parade of supernatural creatures that rode across the land at night.

This chalk horse, carved on a hillside in Britain 3,000 years ago, may represent the Celtic horse-goddess Epona.

In Celtic art, Cernunnos the shape-changer god, was shown as both a horned man and a stag.

Celtic Tales

Celtic peoples honored warrior heroes and told thrilling legends about them—stories of battles, cattle raids, and brave deeds. A Welsh tale tells of Brân the Blessed, a giant hero who fought against the Irish. When Brân was badly wounded, he told his warriors to cut off his head and take it with them. To their amazement, Brân's head could talk! It was buried at the White Mount, later the site of the Tower of London, where it protected Great Britain against invasion.

The geological formation known as the Giant's Causeway is thought to have been the inspiration for one of the legends of Finn MacCool.

A famous Irish Celtic hero is Finn MacCool. One day, Finn was insulted by a giant who lived across the sea in Scotland. In order to reach him, angry Finn hurled pieces of the cliff into the sea, forming a mighty highway that still exists today. Another Irish warrior hero was Cuchulain (koo-KUL-un). When Cuchulain was wounded in battle, he fastened himself to a stone column and fought on until he died fighting.

In one battle, Cuchulain, a fierce warrior, was forced to kill a good friend.

The Legend of King Arthur

Perhaps the most famous Celtic tale is the British legend of King Arthur. Arthur, the son of a king, was raised by a wizard named Merlin. When he came of age, Arthur pulled a sword from a stone, proving that he was the rightful king.

With his Knights of the Round Table, Arthur brought peace to his country. Unfortunately, Arthur's beautiful wife Guinevere (GWEN-uh-veer) fell in love with his bravest knight, Sir Lancelot. Heavy-hearted, Arthur went to war against Lancelot. Meanwhile, his son, Mordred, plotted against him and seized the throne. Arthur defeated Mordred, but was fatally wounded. As he lay dying, three mysterious women appeared in a barge and took him to the Isle of Avalon. It is said that in a time of great need, Arthur will return to rescue his people.

Arthur's sword was named Excalibur, which in Celtic means "hard lightning."

This ancient broadsword is like one Arthur might have used.

The Round Table was inscribed with the names of Arthur's knights.

The *Eisteddfod* festival promotes Welsh poetry and storytelling.

Celtic Storytelling

Celtic tales were first written down by monks hundreds of years ago. Celtic storytellers, called bards, also passed tales down through the generations. Bards went through long training. They were not only storytellers, but also musicians, poets, and historians. Today, a Welsh annual festival, called the *Eisteddfod* (is-TETH-vohd), celebrates this tradition of poetry, music, and tales.

Irish and Scottish storytellers called *seanachie* (SHAWN-ah-kee) retold the histories of families and places, as well as tales. Stories are still shared at local gatherings called *cèilidh* (KAY-lee), along with singing and dancing. Modern storytelling festivals are also springing up in many places in Ireland. Through events like these, the fantastic stories of the past are preserved for future generations.

Storytellers such as Ireland's Pat Speight pass on Celtic tales to the next generation.

One modern-day *seanachie* named Scot AnSgeulaiche put it this way: "There are many ways to come to an understanding of ourselves. The tales are one. A powerful one."

31

Index